Islam:
Beginners Guide to Understanding Islam & the Sunni Shia Schism

Darrell D. Culbertson

Disclaimer & Copyright

Table of Contents

Introduction

Islam is one of the most popular religion in the world with over 1 billion followers worldwide. As with any other widespread religions, many different schisms and sects have emerged over the course of history so that Islam has come to be interpreted in many different ways.

Of those schisms, the split between the Sunnis and Shiites has been by far the oldest and most enduring split. Because it occurred approximately 1,400 years ago, the causes and consequences have become blurred.

Today, myths and confusion abound and few people—even within the Muslim community itself—actually know what really happened and what that really means for today's world.

This book has been written with the intention of clearing up that confusion. It is primarily intended for readers who are not very familiar with Islam in general—let alone the actual significance of the split between Sunni and Shiite—who are interested in learning more.

Knowing the history of the religion and the current tensions in the Middle East will go a long way toward helping you understand the complexity and nuance of the situation.

In the following 6 chapters, you will gain a much deeper understanding of the Sunnis and the Shiites as well as Islam more broadly. Some of the features of this book include:

- An overview of the belief system and structure of the Islamic religion

- The geography, politics, and daily life of believers in Islam

- A history of the rise of Islam in the Arabic world

- A detailed discussion of the Sunni Shia schism

- A closer look at the Sunni belief system, geography, politics, and daily life

- A closer look at the Shiite belief system, geography, politics, and daily life

- Deeper analysis of the present day conflicts, including differing perspectives on its origins and roots.

While reading just one book cannot make an you expert on the situation, this book will allow you to view the news coming out of the Middle East from a much more informed perspective and give you the foundation you need to do further research and learn more.

Chapter 1: An Overview of Islam, Part I: The Belief System

If you are familiar with Christian or Jewish beliefs, then you already have a basic understanding of Islam. The religion is actually an outgrowth of the former. In overly simplistic terms, Muslims believe that God chose the prophet Muhammad to be the final prophet and the deliverer of the correct and most accurate word of God.

In essence, they do not wholly discount what is written in the Torah or the Bible but do believe that it has been changed or altered over the years so that it no longer represents the absolute and true word of God.

Regardless, the God in Islam is the same God in either Christianity or Judaism so that it is not an entirely different religious system—such as Hinduism or Taoism—but a differing belief in the correct way to worship God and the structure of the history and principles as told through written texts.

Muslims believe that Islam is the complete and pure version of the same faith which was revealed to Adam, Noah, and the other prophets. However, they believe the earlier transmissions of that same faith were partially misinterpreted or altered over time. Because of this, Muhammad was needed in order to record the true and unaltered version of faith in the form of the Qur'an.

In this chapter, we'll take a quick look at the main tenants of Islam and the foundations of this belief system.

Islamic Understanding of God

Islam is, above all, a monotheistic religion—meaning they believe that there is one God rather than many. While this holds true for both Judaism and Christianity, Islam emphasizes this point much more firmly. From the perspective of Islam, even the Christian belief in the divine trinity or the idea that anyone aside from God could possess any degree of divinity is blasphemous.

So, while Islam does believe that Jesus and all of the other people discussed in the Torah and in the Bible existed, the perspective is different. The most important distinction being that Jesus is not seen as the son of God but one prophet in a long chain of prophets which ended with Muhammad, who was the final prophet. Thus, Jesus was simply human and possessed no divine power.

Because there is just one God who is incomparable and incomprehensible, Muslims are discouraged from attempting to visualize God. This is the fundamental reason for the conflicts we've seen in recent history with Muslim communities becoming outraged by non-Muslims drawing images of God or Muhammad (both of whom should not be visualized).

Since no human can possess divinity, Muslims do not depend on intermediaries to communicate the word of

God to them or to communicate their prayers to God. Religious clerics provide guidance and leadership but are not believed to possess some special connection with God as a priest or the pope in Catholicism.

This means that a Muslim's relationship with God is extremely personal. They communicate directly through prayer whenever they are in need.

Finally, Muslims also believe that the sole purpose of existence is to worship God. In order to do this, they must practice the 5 pillars of their faith which are discussed in the next section.

The 5 Pillars of Islam

Creed

Islam has a basic creed which states that the person who recites is dedicating his or her life to the service and worship of God. It is a specific statement which must be recited under oath. Muslims repeat it during the daily prayers. It is also said by those wishing to convert to Islam during the conversion process.

The repetition of the creed is meant to serve as a constant reminder of one's purpose in life as a Muslim.

Daily Prayers

Islam has a much more involved ritual when compared to say, protestant Christianity. Muslims must pray 5 times each day. These times are fixed, and the process of praying is highly specific.

→ Flags: De Salon - all of your day is a prayer.

Specific verses of the Qur'an must be recited in the original Arabic. While praying, the believer's chest must be facing the Kaaba located in Mecca. The Kaaba is a small cube-shaped building in the center of the mosque in Mecca (Saudi Arabia). It is considered to be the house of God and is the most sacred site in the Islam religion.

These rituals of regular daily prayers are meant to focus the mind and strengthen one's faith and duty to God. They are also often used as times to engage in personal communication with God.

Almsgiving

Almsgiving is one of the most progressive aspects of the Islamic faith. All Muslims above a certain income level are required to give a fixed portion of their wealth to the poor and needy each year.

2) similar to Mormon

This is not voluntary as church donations are in Christian faiths. It is an obligation for all who can afford it. Furthermore, all of the money goes directly to helping the poor and needy rather than to funding the mosque or paying the clerics.

According to Islam, the wealth of those who are well-off does not belong to them. Rather, it is granted to them as a trust from God's bounty and Muslims believe that God intends them to use that wealth to do his will—in this case, support those who are in need.

The amount required is typically set at 2.5% of your capital assets (money) each year. However, it is strongly encouraged to give more than that if you can.

Almsgiving has played a key role in the maintenance of society. In fact, it is in Islamic areas where we see the first signs of what one might call a "welfare state" today.

Almsgiving in Islam is so well-established that it actually provides approximately 15x more funding for the less fortunate than all global humanitarian aid contributions put together.

This, along with other Islamic principles regarding money and business has had an important—and often positive—impact on social and economic conditions in areas where Islam is the dominant religion.

Ramadhan Fasting

Ramadhan is one of the most important holidays in Islam. It occurs during the 9th month of the Islamic calendar and is observed throughout the entire month. The holiday commemorates the first revelation given to Muhammad.

Muslims are expected to fast every day from dawn until dusk during this month. They cannot eat or drink while the sun is up. This fasting is meant to encourage a feeling of closeness to God. It is also a way of expressing one's gratitude for and dependence on God as well as atone for past sins.

Muslims are also meant to think of the less-fortunate during this time meaning that there is usually an increase in charitable donations and actions during this time.

Islam does not mandate fasting for those who would be unduly burdened or harmed by doing it. However, for all able-bodied people, this is a fundamental necessity, and it is a great sin to break the fast during daylight.

Pilgrimage to Mecca

The final pillar of the 5 pillars of Islam is the pilgrimage to Mecca in Saudi Arabia. All able-bodied Muslims are required to make at least one pilgrimage to the site in their lifetime.

This is not simply a matter of traveling to the site and visiting the mosque. It is much more involved. Along the journey, Muslims are required to stop at specific sites and spend a specific amount of time sleeping in tents in the dessert or even out in the open. This ritual is meant to replicate the journey that Abraham himself took.

They must also stop in Jamarat to symbolically stone the devil by flinging pebbles at three walls in the city of Mina.

Once they reach Mecca, they must walk around the Kaaba seven times. Then, they must walk between Mount Safa and Mount Marwah seven times. This latter ritual is meant to replicate Abraham's wife when she went in search of water for her son, Ismael.

Islamic Understanding of Angels & Prophets

In Islam, both angels and prophets play central roles. The word for angel in Arabic, *Malak* literally translates as messenger. This is in reference to their role as messengers of God. They communicate revelations from God to the human prophets.

Angels are also responsible for recording the actions of human beings and taking the soul when a person dies. As in Christianity and Judaism, angels do not possess free will, so they serve God in total obedience. This is in contrast to humans who do have free will and, therefore, are able to choose whether or not to serve God.

Unlike angels, prophets are human. They do not possess any divine powers although they can sometimes perform miracles in order to prove their claim to others.

In Islam, Adam, Noah, Abraham, Moses, and all the others that you can find in Judaism and Christianity are regarded as prophets. Jesus is also considered a prophet.

Muhammad is the final prophet and, as such plays a key role in Islam as the one who delivered the final revelation and true, unaltered word of God.

The Qur'an

The Qur'an is the key religious text in Islam, fulfilling much the same role as the Bible in Christian faiths and the Torah in Judaism. It is believed to be the absolute and final word of God which God transmitted to people through Muhammad.

Muslims believe that, over time, the previous texts (Torah and Bible) had become distorted and, as a result, the practices of Christianity and Judaism were seen as misguided.

God told his final revelations to Muhammad in order that Muhammad would give the true, undistorted word of God to the people, and they would be able to practice their faith and worship God correctly.

The Qur'an was not written by Muhammad, however. It was written, instead, by his companions. Muhammad is said to have received a series of revelations from God, via the archangel Gabriel, over the span of his final 22 years of life. Upon receiving a revelation, he would tell it to his companions who would write it down.

In total, there are 6,236 verses in the Qur'an which are divided into 114 chapters. It is widely considered to be the finest example of literary work in Arabic.

Muslims are so concerned with distortion and misinterpretation that they do not even considered translated version of the Qur'an to be actual scriptures. Only the original Arabic text is considered valid scripture. All translations are seen as universally insufficient and are regarded as commentaries on the religion rather than actual scripture.

The original Arabic language Qur'an, then, is used as both a moral guide and a sort of instruction manual on how to live one's life in accordance with Islamic principles and values.

In addition to the Qur'an, there is a second text known as the Hadith. It is a record of Muhammad's life. This is not considered to be the word of God but it is used as a supplement to assist in interpreting the Qur'an.

Resurrection & Judgement

Muslims believe that there will be a day of resurrection in which the prophets will return. On this day, all of humanity will be judged by their actions and assigned to go either to heaven or to hell based on that judgment.

The exact time this will happen has already been preordained by God, but it is not (and cannot be) known by any human.

While there are many actions which are considered sinful and will result in the person going to hell according to Islamic belief, it is possible to repent and be cleansed of your sins just as one can repent in Christianity.

Chapter 2: An Overview of Islam, Part II: Geography, Politics & Everyday Life

Now that you have a better understanding of the actual tenants of the faith, let's take a look at Islam on the ground. Who is Muslim? Where do they live? What are their daily lives like?

Understanding this is essential to understanding the split between the Sunni and Shia. All of the beliefs mentioned in the previous chapter are shared by both groups. However, there are key differences in how this belief plays out in everyday practice.

In this chapter, we'll look at the demographics and geography (including breakdown based on Sunni and Shia). We'll also look at how Islam affects economics, diet, family life, and even clothing. Here, there will also be differences between Sunni and Shia.

However, those differences are minor. The key point at which the Sunni and Shia differ is more a political matter than a matter of interpreting the word of God or even religious practice. This will be discussed in greater detail later. In order to understand the important differences—as well as the consequences of those differences—it's first necessary to learn the smaller divergences as well as their shared history and beliefs.

Demographics & Geographical Spread

Altogether, Muslims make up nearly a quarter (23%) of the total global population. There are an estimated 1.62 billion followers spread out over the world. Although it originally started in the Middle East where Muhammad first started spreading his teachings, that is not actually where the highest concentration of Muslims is located.

In fact, of the 1.62 billion followers, 25% live in South Asia. Another 20% live in the Middle East and 15% live in Sub Saharan Africa. The rest are spread out across the globe in Europe, the United States, South America, Australia, and everywhere else.

Sunni & Shia Demographics

While there are no definite figures, Sunni Muslims are definitely in the overwhelming majority. By the best estimates, approximately 80% to 85% of Muslims are Sunni. The remaining 15% to 20% are Shia.

Despite being in the minority, Shia Muslims still exert power and influence in key regions. In the Middle East, they dominate the Persian Gulf. They are the overwhelming majority in Iran and form a significant majority of the population in both Iraq and Azerbaijan as well. Shia Muslims make up around half of the population of Yemen. They form a strong minority in Turkey, Syria, Afghanistan, the United Arab Emirates and Pakistan.

Sunnis dominate the rest of the Middle East and the world. An important thing to note about this distribution of population is that, while forming the minority of the total Muslim population, they are the dominant population in those key countries that possess the largest supplies of oil.

With oil such a precious commodity at the moment, this gives Shia Muslims considerable political power despite otherwise being a minority. As we will discuss later on when we look at the current state of the Sunni Shia divide, this fact plays an important role in the current state of affairs.

An Economy Based on Islamic Principles

The almsgiving you read about in chapter 1 is an important and fundamental feature of Islamic Economics. But there are also many other principles found in the Qur'an and the Hadith that guide the economy. Taken altogether, these principles greatly improved the social status of many people who had previously been exploited and treated in degrading and dehumanizing ways.

For example, Islam sets clear guidelines regarding inheritance and wealth in the family. Previously, men had full control over the household's money. Even if women brought in money, the man determined how it was spent. Under Islam, women had full right of ownership over their own wealth.

In a marriage, the dowry which used to be paid to the father now had to be paid to the wife. Afterward, the husband had no say as to what the wife did with her dowry.

Upon a father's death, women now had a right to inheritance. Previously, woman could not inherit wealth and would be passed over for any sons. Under Islam, daughters were able to inherit 50% of the amount any sons inherited and she could not be passed over for a younger brother.

Islam places great importance on reducing the gap between the rich and the poor. This is, in large part, why the practices regarding women and wealth were included.

In addition, there is a strict rule against interest bearing loans. Throughout Europe and the United States (and many other parts of the world), taking out a loan means you agree to pay back the principal amount of the loan plus an additional percentage of interest.

This is not allowed under Islamic law. All loans must be interest-free. In terms of taxes, wealth may be taxed but trade may not. This means that sales tax and other similar taxes are forbidden. Income tax, on the other hand, is used.

Furthermore, it is strongly discouraged to hoard wealth. That is, the practice of accumulating large quantities of wealth without spending it and keeping it in circulation in the economy is considered immoral. On a similar note, hoarding food for the purpose of speculation—waiting for the price to bump up—is illegal.

Taxes which are collected by the state must be immediately used to help the poor. Because of this requirement, Islamic states became the earliest cases of what we might call "welfare states" today. They provided social security for both the elderly and children.

They provided financial support to poor families and mandated that employers provide health care for their employee. It is also significant to note that this mandatory health care also applied to slave owners regarding their slaves (making Islam by far the most progressive religion at the time regarding slavery).

Halal: Dietary Restrictions

Before we discuss dietary restrictions, it is important to note that the term "halal" refers to all objects or actions that are permissible according to Islam. It is actually one of five categories which are used to define human actions according to their relative morality. The five categories include:

1. Fard (Compulsory)

2. Mustahabb (Recommended)

3. Halal (Allowed)

4. Makruh (Disliked)

5. Haram (Forbidden)

Using these categories, the morality of all human behavior is codified according to Islamic values. With that in mind, halal is perhaps most often used in reference to the dietary restrictions which exist in Islam.

Here is a quick overview of the dietary guidelines—guidelines which both Sunni and Shia follow:

1. No alcohol

2. No pork

3. No blood

4. No carnivorous animals

5. All permissible meats must be prepared according to a specific Halal practice (regarding the raising and slaughtering of the animal which should be done by a Muslim).

6. Meat that was hunted or fished by you can be eaten despite not being slaughtered according to the specific halal method.

7. Carrion (i.e. – carcasses of animals that died in the wild)

In Shia Islam, there is an ongoing debate about whether it is permissible to eat meats slaughtered by Christians or Jews. This is because their techniques do not technically follow the halal method. While Sunni Muslims widely believe that it is still permissible even if the meat has not been prepared by a Muslim (so long as it is not pork or carrion), Shia are divided as to whether or not it is allowed.

In the Qur'an, an exception to these rules is made in the case that there is absolutely no halal food available. If under threat of starvation, a Muslim is allowed to eat non-halal food in order to prevent death.

Family Life

In Islam, as in Christianity and Judaism, the essential unit is the nuclear family. It is widely known that Islam permits men to have multiple wives. What is less known is that this is simply a compromise with the practices that existed in the area prior to the introduction of Islam.

We will go into more details in the next chapter but for the time being, it's important to point out that before Islam, men would take as many wives as they wanted and divorce them just as easily. As women had no status or influence on their own, this often meant they were subject to terrible conditions and, if divorced, relegated to poverty and shame.

In an attempt to elevate the status of women and prevent men from exploiting them, Islam sets very rigorous guidelines for marriage. Men can only take a maximum of 4 wives. More importantly, they must provide for and treat each wife equally (and adequately). If they cannot afford to provide for 4 wives equally well, they cannot have that many wives.

Furthermore, men cannot simply divorce a woman just because they've found another woman they find more pleasing. Divorce was made more difficult in order to prevent women from being abandoned to a life of poverty.

Violence against one's spouse or children is also strictly discouraged. Muslims are instructed to manage their anger and emotions and express them calmly rather than resorting to violence.

It is also important to note that although polygamy is permitted (provided the strict requirements are met), the vast majority of Islamic marriages are monogamous.

In regard to children, Islam banned the practice of killing female newborns and abolished the system in which children were regarded as the property of their father. Under Islam, children now had much more independence, could not be used as forced labor, and could not be sold off into marriages without their own consent.

Thus, family life was greatly improved in many ways by the introduction of Islam. Of course, it is important to understand that simply introducing a new set of rules will not immediately change the actual practices and behaviors, it would take decades before the principles and values of Islam would become widespread practice in everyday life.

When viewed from today, many of the guidelines regarding family and everyday life might be seen as outdated or not progressive enough. However, the same could be said for most religions. One must remember to consider the historical context in which holy scriptures were written. When viewed from thousands of years in the future, any text will seem outdated.

The Myths & Realities of Jihad

There are many misconceptions surrounding the concept of Jihad in Islam. According to many outsiders, it is believed that jihad strictly refers to religiously motivated war or acts of violence. Many also believe that such war and violence is mandated by the religion. This leads to the misconception that Islam is an inherently violent religion.

In reality, this couldn't be further from the mark. The Qur'an is overwhelmingly concerned with advocating peace, encouraging a sense of community which transcends race, ethnicity, and even religion, and encouraging compassion and generosity.

With that said, jihad is an important concept in Islam. However, it doesn't just refer to religiously motivated war. So let's break down this concept. The literal translations of the Arabic "jihad" in English is "to strive or struggle" in the way of God.

This struggle can be categorized as either "greater Jihad" or "lesser Jihad." Greater jihad is the individual's struggle toward spiritual self-perfection.

That is, striving to follow the moral guidelines in the Qur'an; striving to dedicate one's life to the worship and service of God, and so on.

Less Jihad refers to warfare. In Islam, warfare is forbidden unless it is for a noble (religious) purpose. Prior to Islam, the Arabic world was fraught with tribal clashes and bloody family feuds. Under Islam, warfare should only be used in order to defend Islam against those who insult or threaten it. This includes non-believers and non-Muslims but also Muslim combatants.

Within the Muslim community, there is serious debate as to what constitutes a real insult or threat to Islam. This has led to the emergence of small (but violent and well-armed) groups of extremists who justify their violent actions by calling it jihad.

In Shia Islam, lesser jihad (war) can only be carried out under the direct leadership of the Imam while Sunni Muslims base Jihad on a more individual basis. This is not to say that Sunni Muslims are exclusively responsible for all war and violence in the Middle East. Shia Muslims certainly can be found in the middle of the conflict.

The distinctions and definitions are hotly debated within and between Sunni and Shia groups. Those with an inclination toward violence will find a way to justify it, whether or not that justification is agreed to by other members of the community. This is why it is important not to view extremist groups as representative of the religion as a whole.

Sharia Law

Outside of the Muslim world, the idea of Sharia law is often invoked to inspire fear. However, the reality looks a lot different than the popular image of women being stoned for adultery.

Sharia law simply refers to laws based on the morals and principles found in the Qur'an (and the Hadith). A group of Islamic scholars are tasked with the job determining which laws should be applied to society and how to make rulings on specific court cases based on the morals and values of Islam.

The modern concept of sharia law emerged in the 9th century when scholars decided that it should be rooted in 4 fundamental areas (ranked in order of importance):

1. Qur'an

2. Hadith

3. The consensus of the Muslim jurists

4. Analogical reasoning

It is important to note that rulings are never written down or codified. Each ruling is made on a case by case basis, and it is made very clear that these rulings are the judgment of men, not judgments made by God. That is, there is a strong emphasis on remembering that sharia law is, at is root, a human attempt at interpreting how Islamic values should be applied to daily life and legal matters.

The rulings made are considered interpretations of the Qur'an, not divinely ordained law. The Qur'an and Hadith are complete and perfect. Human interpretation of them, however, can be incomplete and flawed. Therefore, rulings should not be made into codified laws because then they might be seen as infallible and divine as the actual scriptures.

Because neither the Qur'an nor the Hadith does not directly reference every single possible human action or legal issue, Sharia law differs from region to region. In cases where there is no direct reference to be found, jurists do their best to infer from other parts of the Qur'an and Hadith in order to make their best guess as to how to decide on the case.

In many cases, non-Muslims are not subject to Sharia law even if they are living in a state where it is used. Often, separate courts are established for non-Muslims.

Sharia law covers all aspects of law including matters of state, foreign relations, daily life, marriage, restitution for injuries and murder, and so on. It also includes rules for fasting, prayer, and charity. According to sharia law, punishments can be applied to the following 5 crimes:

1. Highway robbery
2. Theft

3. Consumption of Alcohol

4. Unlawful intercourse

5. False accusation of unlawful intercourse

Most Muslim groups adhere to Sharia law even if they are not living in a state which uses it at the national level.

Chapter 3: A History of Islam, Part I: Pre-Islamic Arabia & the Time of Muhammad

In order to truly understand Islam and the impact it has had on history and its believers, it's important to have a clear understanding of its cultural context. Many people today will criticize Islamic beliefs as extreme or oppressive. However, when understood within the context of the time they emerged, they are actually considerably progressive.

In some cases, Islamic principles were even more progressive than those of other religious systems—especially with regard to slavery and women's rights. In order for that to become clear, then, let's set the stage and learn what life was like in the Arabic world before Muhammad began spreading the ideas and beliefs of Islam.

Pre-Islamic Arabic World

Islam rose in the early 7th century with Muhammad. Before that, the Arabian peninsula was populated by multiple warring clans and civilizations with differing religious beliefs. Some believed in an indigenous polytheistic religion while others practiced Judaism, Christianity, or Zoroastrianism. Christianity—specifically Nestorian Christianity—was dominant in the eastern part where Islam would first get its start.

By the early 7th century, the Arabic region was deeply engulfed in a long and destructive war with the Byzantine Empire and the Sassanid Empire. At the same time, a plague was ravaging the area, killing tens of thousands of people.

Society was heavily segregated into classes of royalty, nobles, the poor, and slaves making life difficult for the overwhelming majority of people (who were either poor or enslaved). These lower classes were heavily exploited by the wealthier elite. Women had no status or rights and were treated as property to be sold or traded. Marriages were arranged without the consent of the woman and in some cases, without the consent of either person to be married.

Because of the lower status of women, female newborns—who were seen as worthless and a financial burden—would often be killed. The elite would force the poor into indentured servitude by granting loans with exorbitant interest rates that could never be repaid.

Contracts would regularly be broken, and both murder and theft were rampant problems. Slaves who lacked even the status of human and were considered property would be murdered without restitution or treated so poorly that they died from the severe conditions.

Men would take multiple wives but tended to treat them poorly and would often divorce them with little cause. Without status or economic opportunities, divorce often meant death or at least poverty for a woman who was no longer considered marriageable after already being "used" by another man.

Likewise, children were considered the property of their father and could be used for labor or sold off in marriages or other trade agreements with other men.

Men, as heads of their households, had free reign to abuse their wives and children without fear of punishment. All told, life was extremely difficult with little hope of escape for the large majority of the population due to the social structures which existed in the region.

This is the world that Muhammad was born into and would grow up in. Many of the revelations he is said to have received from God were specifically addressing these hardships and social problems.

The Life & Times of Muhammad

Muhammad was likely born in 570 CE (the exact year is unconfirmed). He was orphaned at a very young age and would ultimately be raised by his uncle, Abu Talib. Before the revelations from God he is said to have received, he worked as a merchant.

While a merchant, he would often retreat to a cave to have solitude and pray. According to the Islamic beliefs, Muhammad began receiving revelations from God via the archangel Gabriel in 610 CE. He would continue to receive these revelations until his death in 632 CE. As the story goes, he would receive a set of revelations, memorize them, and then recite them to his companions who would then write them down.

These written records would later be collected together to form the Qur'an. Altogether, he would recite 6,236 verses which would be divided into 114 chapters spanning every topic from the meaning of life to instructions for everyday life.

Muhammad preached these revelations to the people in Mecca and implored them to abandon the polytheistic beliefs they currently followed. While he did gain a few followers at this time, the majority would not convert, and the authorities in Mecca persecuted him.

As a result of this persecution, he and his small group of followers migrated to Abyssinia where they would continue to spread their beliefs. The earliest converts to Islam were often poor or enslaved people who took solace in the religion's emphasis on compassion and generosity toward the less fortunate.

Many of the elites at the time, however, were displeased with Muhammad and his teachings. They accused him of destabilizing the social order by teaching the poor and enslaved that they deserved better as well as by advocating racial equality.

Muhammad's followers grew slowly but surely. By 616 or 617 CE, the Banu Hashim clan would sympathize with Islam and began protecting Muhammad from those who wanted him dead or, at the very least, imprisoned and punished.

Two other clans—Makhzum and Banu Abd Sham— would declare a boycott against Banu Hashim in an attempt to force them to stop protecting Muhammad. The boycott lasted 2 or 3 years but failed to achieve its goal.

However, by the time the boycott ended, it had already caused considerable strain and hardship for Muhammad and his family. His wife, Khadijah, and his uncle, Abu Talib would die shortly after the boycott was ended as a result of the damage to their health that resulted from it.

619 CE, the year the boycott ended and the year that Muhammad's wife and uncle died, would forever be remembered in history as the Year of Sorrow.

A few years later, in 622 CE, Muhammad would immigrate to Medina—an event which would later become known as the Hijra. There, he built a state and established political and religious authority. He would also create the Constitution of Medina which declared all Islamic people to be a member of the same community (*ummah*) regardless of nationality, ancestry, race, or geography.

The constitution would also establish greater religious freedom, improve the status of both women and slaves, and set a judicial system (which included the ability of non-Muslims to be judged according to their own laws).

Over the next few years, Muhammad and his followers would become mired in a series of battles. In 629 CE, he would finally succeed in his conquest of Mecca—the place which had previously persecuted and pressured him to leave years before.

By his death in 632 CE, Muhammad had successfully united the tribes of Arabia into a single polity under Islam. This is all the more impressive considering the extreme animosity and the frequency of war and violence which had existed before.

According to Islamic beliefs, Muhammad would be the final prophet and the collection of revelations he taught (the Qur'an) would be the complete and final true word of God.

Chapter 4: A History of Islam, Part II: From Muhammad's Death to Present Day

After Muhammad died in 632 CE, the question immediately arose of who would (and should) succeed him—not as a prophet, but as leader of the Muslim community. To resolve the issue, the caliphate was established, and it is here that we first see the beginnings of a split within the Muslim community into what would later become known as the Sunni and Shia.

The caliphate is a system of government—with the head position being known as the caliph. The caliphate is meant to act as both political and religious leader of the Muslim community, with no clear distinction between religion and state as is seen in other parts of the world like the United States and Europe.

Thus, the vacuum of power that Muhammad left when he died had been filled, or so it seemed. The question still remained of who should be caliph. That is, how should the caliph be chosen?

The vast majority agreed that the caliph should be elected via consensus by the community. However, a small but still significant minority of the Muslim community believed that the caliph should be a blood relative of Muhammad and that Islam should continue throughout history to be led by Muhammad's bloodline and his bloodline alone.

Here the cracks begin to form which would eventually become a chasm permanently dividing Sunni (the majority who were in favor of election) and the Shia (the minority who were in favor of keeping with Muhammad's bloodline).

Ultimately, Abu Bakr would be elected as the first caliph to succeed Muhammad. He was not a blood relative of Muhammad and so was not seen as a legitimate leader by the Shia minority. He would die two years later in 634. Three more caliphs would succeed him, and this group of the 4 first caliphs would become known by the Sunnis as the Rashidun Caliphate, which translates as "the rightly guided" Caliphs.

The fourth of these, Ali ibn Abi Talib, was a descendent of Muhammad and, therefore, would become the first caliph to be acknowledged by the Shia minority. However, as they do not believe the process of choosing the caliphate, they would adopt their own system in which the leader of the community is referred to as the Imam. Thus, Ali ibn Abi Talib, while being the 4th caliphate would also become the 1st imam.

More details about these early years immediately after Muhammad's death will be given in the next chapter when we take a much closer look at how this schism between Sunni and Shia formed and how it developed over this time period.

For now, we will just take a quick and broad look at the history of Islam from the time of Muhammad's death up to present day. This is a time frame spanning 1,400 years, so this will be a very broad strokes overview.

After Ali ibn Abi Talib, Sunni Muslims would continue to use the election process for choosing the caliph. At the same time, Shia Muslims would continue to follow the descendants of Muhammad whom they referred to as imams.

By the middle of the 1300s, the Ottoman Empire was on the rise. Murad I, king of the Ottoman Empire, would claim the title of Caliph for himself and the seat of the caliphate would be moved to Edirne, the capital of the Ottoman Empire.

The king of the Ottoman Empire would continue to also act as the Caliph of the Muslim community throughout its existence until it fell in 1924 after World War I.

In that year, Mustafa Kemal—the first president of the newly formed Turkish Republic—would completely abolish the position of Caliph as part of larger secular reforms which attempted to separate religion from state.

Since then, attempts have been made to revive the position, and many Sunni Muslims regard the existence of a caliphate as desirable. This is because the Arabic world enjoyed a long history of prosperity, scientific advancement, and progress throughout the 1,400-year long succession of caliphs.

Some extremist groups such as ISIL (or, alternatively, ISIS) not only demand the reinstatement of the caliphate but have actually established a caliphate of their own. The legitimacy of these self-established caliphates usually is not recognized outside of the groups themselves.

Beyond the issue of the caliphate, the Muslim population has grown substantially since its humble origins in Mecca. As you read earlier, Islam now dominates as the world's most populated religion. With over 1 billion followers, it has spread out of the Middle East and onto every continent—save Antarctica, of course.

Since the 1960s, a growing number of Muslims from around the world have begun to immigrate to Europe and the United States for economic reasons. The host nations tend to welcome them with anxiety and suspicion.

As oil became an increasingly important commodity throughout the 20th century, tensions in the Middle East have grown. The United States and Europe both have a vested interest in the resource and have, as a result, become deeply entangled in the complex interrelations that exist between Sunni and Shia, between Muslim and non-Muslim and between different nations in the region.

The political and social reality of the area is complex and extremely nuanced. If you are reading this book, it is likely because you already have an idea of how complex it is and wish to understand it at least a little bit better.

Whatever can be said for the wars and military interventions that have been done in the Middle East—largely by the United States but with the help of Europe—it is becoming more and more apparent that a greater understanding of the situation on the ground is needed. These conflicts have dragged on for decades largely because these foreign interests dove into the middle without a clear understanding of what was going on or how the situation might best be handled.

This ongoing presence of foreign military powers which lack a sufficient understanding of the situation has worked to intensify the conflict further and deepen the divide which exists between Sunni and Shia.

Now that you have a strong foundation in the history and beliefs of Islam as a whole, you are ready to dig finally into the finer details of the Sunni and Shia divide. In the next chapter, we'll take a much closer look at how the divide began, how it developed over time, and what the consequences of it have been.

Afterward, you'll get a full chapter devoted to the beliefs and views which are unique to the Sunni Muslims followed by a full chapter about the beliefs and views unique to Shia Muslims. In the final chapter, we'll look at the current state of the Sunni Shia divide and how that relates to the modern conflicts we see in the Middle East.

Chapter 5: The Sunni & Shia Schism – A Closer Look

The story of the Sunni & Shia split is long. However, it is important to note that it is not the story of relentless and unyielding violence. Throughout the 1,400 years in which the schism existed, Sunni and Shia have lived side by side peacefully for the majority of that time.

With that said, this history has been marked by moments of tension and conflict which played an important role in widening the existing schism and ensuring that Sunni and Shia would never again join as one group although they would successfully live side by side for centuries.

632 to 661 CE – the First 4 Caliphs (Rashidun Caliphate)

The period immediately after Muhammad's death until 680 would see the most conflict between Sunni and Shia until the 20th century. The Sunni and Shia disagreed about how to choose his successor and with each caliph, the decision would meet with increasing opposition.

The Sunni, who were in the majority, thought that the successor should be elected by consensus of the Muslim community. The small Shia minority, on the other hand, thought that Muhammad's successor should descend from Muhammad's own bloodline. As the majority, the Sunni would have their way and the first Caliph would be Abu Bakr, a close friend (but not relative) of Muhammad. His successors would continue to be chosen by the community—according to the Sunni method—despite the growing opposition of the Shia minority.

This would, in 680 CE, culminate in the Battle of Karbala. After that, Sunni and Shia would live in relative harmony and without major conflicts for about 800 years. In 1500 CE, the Shia dominant Safavid Empire would rise and conquer Persia. However, after the initial takeover, the Safavid Empire would live peacefully alongside the Ottoman Empire with the exception of some clashes between the two.

After the Safavid Empire was ended in the 18th century, Sunni and Shia would again continue to live together under Ottoman rule, even attending the same mosques and praying together.

Let's take a closer look at each of these events:

Abu Bakr

Abu Bakr would become the first Caliph after Muhammad's death in 632 CE. He was a close friend of Muhammad and one of the companions which wrote down the revelations Muhammad received.

Immediately after being chosen, many of the tribes which Muhammad had managed to unite under the Islamic faith would go back on their oaths, arguing that they had made the oath to Muhammad himself, not to Islam as a whole.

As a result, Abu Bakr would spend the majority of his short reign to restore an Islamic community which had fallen into shambles. He would accomplish this by a series of wars which lasted a full year and became known as the Ridda wars.

He began by dividing his army into several corps which he then sent out to strategically reclaim the weakest tribes which had renounced the religion. After conquering these weaker tribes, he would work his way up, challenging stronger and stronger tribes as his own army grew stronger and stronger. In this way, Abu Bakr systematically re-stitched together the Muslim community which Muhammad had built.

With the work of rebuilding the community done, Abu Bakr would immediately embark on wars of conquest during the second year of his reign. He began in Iraq and then moved into Syria. He would die in 634 but before his death, he had declared his wish for Umar ibn al Khattab to succeed him as caliph because he recognized al Khattab's military and political skill—which would ensure that Abu Bakr's wars of conquest would be continued.

Umar ibn al Khattab

As Abu Bakr wished, Umar ibn al Khattab would be named the second Caliph. He would also continue the wars of conquest by pushing deeper into the Sassanid

Empire in Persia as well as into Egypt and Byzantine territory.

These were all wealthy and powerful centers of the empires to which they belonged. However, because the Sassanid and Byzantine empires had been engaged in extended conflict, both had been left exhausted and vulnerable. This meant the Islamic armies under al Khattab's command would be able to secure an easy victory.

By 640 CE, al Khattab had expanded the Islamic empire greatly. It now encompassed all of Mesopotamia, Syria, and Palestine. By 642, it had absorbed Egypt and by 643, the entire Persian Empire was under its control.

Even as al Khattab was engaged in these successful wars of conquest, he would also work to establish a strong, stable political structure that could effectively administer an empire which was growing rapidly and composed of an increasingly diverse range of people who subscribed to different religions, practiced different customs, and even spoke different languages.

In order to accommodate this diversity and in keeping with the teachings of the Qur'an, al Khattab allowed a relatively high degree of autonomy to local groups. Conquered people were allowed to continue speaking their own language and practice their own customs of social and political life so long as those customs did not conflict with the Islamic rule. In fact, he would even allow the local governments to retain their power except for now being under the authority of an Islamic governor and financial officer who were primarily tasked with collecting taxes.

Christians and Jews who were now subsumed into the Islamic Empire were not forced to convert to Islam. They were not even forced to fight in the Islamic army. Furthermore, non-Muslims would be given the right to be judged under their own laws rather than Islamic law.

In addition to practicing tolerance and taking steps to accommodate the diversity of the Islamic Empire, al Khattab would be the first to establish what would be called a welfare state today. His government would grant retirement pensions to the elderly, provide social security for children, and provide income for the disabled who were unable to work.

This support was available to Muslims and non-Muslims alike and was funded by the taxes collected as well as the wealth acquired through conquest. After al Khattab, the Islamic empire would continue to maintain this policy of social support.

Al Khattab was assassinated in 644 CE during morning prayers by a Persian slave. Before his death, he would establish a committee of six men who should choose the next Caliph from amongst themselves.

Uthman ibn Affan

The third Caliph would be Uthman ibn Affan. During the first half of his reign, he was one of the most popular Caliphs thus far. However, he would meet with increasing opposition during the latter half until he, too, was assassinated.

He immediately carried on the wars of conquest begun by Abu Bakr. Under his reign, the Islamic Empire would conquer the rest of North Africa, Rhodes, Cyprus, the coastal areas of the Iberian Peninsula, and coastal Sicily.

In addition to this expansion of the empire, it would be under his reign that Muhammad's revelations would finally be compiled into a single book which would be called the Qur'an. HE would also add diacritics (accent marks) to the Arabic letters in order to help non-native speakers of Arabic read the scripture more easily.

During the latter half of his reign, a growing movement in Egypt would demand that Ali ibn Abi Talib become Caliph. Protestors surrounded his home to demand his resignation from the seat of Caliph. They also expressed their grievances regarding certain local governors which Uthman had appointed.

Uthman wanted to resolve the disputes through peaceful negotiation and consultation, even admonishing his own people to refrain from violence against the protestors.

Despite this, the protest eventually escalated into a rebellion. His house was set on fire and he was beaten and stabbed to death in 656 CE. This event would polarize the Muslim community as debate arose regarding the religious beliefs about rebellion and governance as well as the qualifications for becoming a leader in Islam.

Ali ibn Abi Talib

The Shia discount the previous three caliphs, arguing that they do not descend from Muhammad and, therefore, were not legitimate caliphs. The fourth caliph, Ali ibn Abi Talib, however, was a different story.

He was the Shia choice in 632 CE when Muhammad had died because he was a direct relative of the prophet. However, he was consistently passed over in favor of the previous 3 caliphs. Finally, he would be chosen as the 4th Caliph. The Shia would declare him to be their first imam—the spiritual and political leader of Shia Muslims.

After the rebellion and assassination of his predecessor, Uthman ibn Affan, Ali would take over as Caliph. He immediately dismissed the governors that the rebels had been displeased with during Uthman's rule. He also moved the capital of the empire from Medina to Kufa (a city which is now in modern day Iraq).

A rebel army soon arose seeking revenge for the assassination of Uthman. The army captured Basra and killed an estimated 4,000 suspected seditionists thought to be involved in the assassination. Ali responded by sending the Caliph's army out but both armies wanted to avoid violence and resolve the matter peacefully.

Despite the desire for peace on both sides, violence broke out between the armies and the Battle of the Camel would take place. This fight between the rebel army and the Caliph's army would become the first fight between Muslims. Ali's army was victorious and put down the rebels.

Afterward, Ali would have to put down many more rebellions and, in the process, lose the support of his people. This significantly weakened the empire and much of the territory which had been won during the previous 3 caliphates would be lost under Ali's caliphate.

He was assassinated in 661 CE by Ibn Muljam as part of a larger plot to assassinate all the different leaders and finally put an end to this civil unrest. His grandson would briefly assume the caliphate after him but would soon agree to cede the position to Mu'awiya in order to restore peaceful relations between the warring groups of Muslims.

680 CE – The Battle of Karbala

After Mu'awiya died, his son, Yazid I, would assume the caliphate. This was met with opposition as the election of his son was seen as an attempt to turn the Caliphate into a familial dynasty. Ali's grandson, Hussein ibn Ali, would refuse to pay allegiance to Yazid I.

He put together a small army to back him and believed that the had the support of the people in Kufa, the capital of the empire. Indeed, he had had support in Kufa but Yazid I had successfully dispersed these supporters. Hussein did not know that Yazid had done this.

In 680 CE, on his way to Kufa to join up with the supporters which he thought were still there, he was intercepted by Yazid's army. They fought and Hussein's army was defeated. The women and children were captured and taken as prisoners.

Beyond these basic facts, the events of this Battle of Karbala are much disputed by the Sunni and Shia. Rather than giving just one story as to what happened, you will be provided with both sides of the story:

Shia Perspective

According to the Shia, Hussein, upon encountering Yazid's army, saw that they were thirsty after days of searching for them. He offered them his storage of water, allowing the entire army, including the horses, to drink.

This significantly diminished his supply. Yazid's army allowed Hussein to set up camp in Karbala but could not let him continue to Kufa. However, the army would not allow Hussein's army to go near the Euphrates. When their water supply began to dwindle, they begged to be allowed to get water from the Euphrates. They were denied.

Hussein sent his brother to get water in spite of the army. His brother's arms were cut off and he was killed. Hussein asked for water to give to his infant son. Instead of providing water, the army launched arrows, killing the infant.

In total, 72 of Hussein's people were killed. The bodies were left for 40 days without burial. Today, the death of these people and, particularly Hussein, is commemorated annually by the Shia in a self-flagellation ritual. Hussein is considered to be a martyr in the Shia faith.

Sunni Perspective

The Sunni dispute this version of the story and deny the entire story about the water. Instead, when the two armies met each other, a commander of Yazid's army approached Hussein. At first, Hussein and his people believed he approached to kill them. Instead, he turned on his own army and fought alongside Hussein. He managed to kill two soldiers before he was killed himself.

The fighting continued until all of Hussein's followers had been killed. Only Hussein himself remained standing. Yazid's soldiers hesitated to kill him at first.

However, one man, Shamar, threw a spear at Hussein. This prompted the rest to kill Hussein. It is said that it was Shamar who beheaded him.

Consequences

The killing of Hussein and the fact the people of Kufa had withdrawn their support of Hussein was criticized by Abd Allah ibn al Zubayr who would establish his authority in Iraq, southern Arabia, parts of Egypt, and a significant portion of Syria.

The Islamic Empire was now divided into two spheres with two different caliphs—or one caliph and one imam—who were I a state of civil war.

Eventually, Abd Allah would lose ground, and his sphere of influence would be reduced to the coastal area of Saudi Arabia, then known as Hejaz. He was killed on the battlefield in 692.

After his death, the Umayyad caliphate would reestablish control, and the empire would once again be united as a whole, recovered from those long decades of rebellion, unrest, and civil war.

941 CE – The Hidden Imam

The history of the hidden imam is not so much a tale of Sunni-Shia conflict as one of Shia religious history. In addition to the disagreement regarding the succession of the Caliphate, Sunni and Shia disagree here on the topic of the Mahdi.

The Mahdi is a sort of messiah or savior who will emerge at some point—already known to God but unknown to humankind—to restore peace and justice to the world. Shia believes that the Mahdi has already been born and is the 12th imam who disappeared in 941 CE. Sunni believe that the Mahdi has not yet been born and, therefore, his identity is not yet known.

However, Sunni and Shia both agree that the Mahdi will be a descendant of the prophet Muhammad. They also largely agree about how he will reemerge, what he will do, and that he will become the universal Caliphate, accepted by Sunni and Shia alike.

According to Shia beliefs and scholarship, the 12th imam is Muhammad ibn Hasan. He is said to be the son of the 11th imam who died when ibn Hasan was just 5 years old, at which point he was appointed as the imam.

There is little known about his life as he spent the majority of it in hiding. It is said that the only appearance he ever made was as a child at his father's funeral. Between 874 (when his father died) and 941, ibn Hasan would remain in hiding but continue to guide the Shia community by sending an instruction to his deputies.

In 941 CE, he would disappear completely in an event which is now referred to as the Major Occultation. The majority of Shia believe that the 12th imam is still alive today and still the leader of the Shia people, but he will not reappear until the time determined by God.

Regardless of the belief that he is still alive, his disappearance left a significant gap in leadership in the Shia community. The imam acted as both a spiritual and religious leader of the community so with his disappearance, they lacked both kinds of leader. At the time, this was not a serious problem since the Shia community had relatively little political power anyway.

However, once Shia dominant states (like Iran and Azerbaijan) began to emerge, issues arose surrounding the role of the state in the Shia community. If the 12th imam is still alive and still the leader of the Shia people, then what role does a Shia government really play in their lives? What validity does that government have when the true leader is the 12th imam? Such questions have caused tension between religion and state in Shia states to this day.

1500 CE – The Safavid Dynasty

The Safavid dynasty came out of what is now Turkey and moved into Persia in order to establish a Shia dominated empire. Before their arrival in 1500 CE, Persia had been the seat of Sunni Islamic scholarship. However, in the 13th century, the Mongolians attacked Persia, destroying many of its schools and libraries in the process.

This led to a large migration of Sunni scholars out of Persia and into Egypt and Anatolia. Their migration left Persia open, and the Shia minority which lived there began converting people to their religion.

By the time the Safavid dynasty, a significant number of Shia already lived in Persia. However, Sunni Muslims still constituted the majority. Immediately after conquering Persia, Ismail I of the Safavid dynasty established Shiism as the official religion of the empire.

Because the majority of the population was still Sunni, Ismail I had to enforce this rule with violence. As a result, the majority either converted or pretended to convert to Shiism. By the 18th century when the Safavid dynasty ended, the majority of the population was genuinely Shia.

The fact that both Iran and Azerbaijan are officially Shia states today is attributed to this period of history in which the Safavid dynasty made every effort to establish Shiism as the dominant religion.

Of the course of their roughly 250-year dynasty, there would be some clashes with the Sunni-dominant Ottoman Empire. However, for the most part, they would live side by side in a tentative state of peace before the dynasty fell and was, ultimately, absorbed by the Ottoman Empire.

This would be the last period of serious conflict between Sunni and Shia until the fall of the Ottoman Empire at the end of World War I. You'll read more about these more modern conflicts in the last chapter of this book.

It has been separated from this older history of the Sunni-Shia divide because these modern conflicts are, arguably, not rooted in the historical Sunni-Shia schism. Instead, the history you have read about in the chapters so far have been used to achieve political or economic goals.

Chapter 6: The Sunni & Shia Schism in Contemporary Times

Today, the two groups continue to be divided. However, the modern face of the conflict and the religion itself have changed as a result of the unique modern circumstances. So, to wrap up the history of this schism, we'll end with a discussion of the complex and nuanced reality which exists today.

First, we'll take a quick look at the state of modern Islam—primarily in the Middle East where it is experiencing the greatest amount of turmoil. Then, we'll examine the modern conflicts between Sunni and Shia. Due to the nature of the topic, there are many perspectives and many conflicting sources of data.

Despite this, one could argue that the modern conflict, while it certainly makes use of the past, is not actually rooted in the original disputes which divided Sunni and Shia all those years ago. Instead, the already existing schism is being used by key political figures in order to achieve political goals. This will be discussed in greater detail later on in this chapter.

Modern Islam

Today, economic migration has spread the Muslim population into new areas. During the height of colonialism in the late 19th and early 20th century, many Muslims would immigrate from India and Indonesia to the Caribbean as indentured servants. A growing number of Muslims would move into Sub-Saharan Africa, Europe, and the United States.

As the influence of secularism in government grew, a movement known as Liberal Islam would emerge which called for a reconciliation of Islamic traditions and secular modes of government. On the other end of the spectrum, some would respond to this secular influence with animosity and establish fundamentalist groups which demanded a revival of purely Islamic government. For these groups, Islam should not just be a religion which guides individuals in their personal lives. They, instead, demand that it also guide social and political life as it had for the preceding millennia.

Many of these fundamentalist groups have become equated with extremist and terrorist acts. While some certainly have committed violent atrocities, there are many who believe in and support the revival of Islamic government without resorting to violent or extremist measures.

Outside of Muslim-dominant countries, the Muslim community has met with increasing persecution and discrimination. Throughout the late 20th century, Muslims experienced persecution and even genocide under Communist regimes in Cambodia, Albania, and China. They were also persecuted in Turkey and Tunisia.

In Europe and the United States, they continue to experience discrimination and prejudice. The global Muslim population is increasingly being judged by (and equated with) the few extremist groups which are committing terrible acts of violence in the Middle East.

A People Re-Divided: Origins & Perspectives of the Modern Conflicts between Sunni and Shia Groups

Since the fall of the Ottoman Empire after World War I which brought with it the end of the Caliphate, the people of the Middle East have struggled to establish stabilized governments. At least partially as a result of the uninformed way the allied powers divided up the regions of the empire which separated communities and forced groups which disagreed with each other to join under one nation.

Under Ottoman rule, local groups enjoyed a relatively high level of autonomy. While they were subjects of the empire, they were allowed to maintain their own laws, language, and customs where they did not conflict with Muslim law. Under the new arrangement of borders and nations established after World War I, this autonomy was taken away, and there was greater pressure for local groups to adopt new governments, new laws, and even new customs.

This created tensions all across the Middle East, tensions which would quickly come to be defined along sectarian Sunni vs. Shia lines in many regions. As oil became an increasingly important resource, the oil-rich Middle East would be further torn apart by fights over the precious resource and foreign interests, primarily the United States and Europe would become increasingly involved in these conflicts.

The period between the end of World War I and 1970 still saw a strong unity between Sunni and Shia as they came together to fight the common threats of colonialism and secularism. While the two sects disagreed about who should hold the position of Caliph, the complete abolition of the Caliphate by allied powers was regarded as a threat to Islam as a whole.

There were protests and movements as far as South Asia in which Sunni and Shia came together to demand the re-establishment of the Caliphate and return to Islamic rule in Muslim countries.

Even in Iran, a Shia dominant nation, efforts were made to accommodate the Sunni minority. The celebration of Muhammad's birthday, for example, became characterized as Islamic unity week and accepted the different dates that Sunni and Shia celebrated his birth.

This relative harmony (relative to present times) would be upset by increasing strife by the 1980s. Increasing tensions and conflicts arising out of nationalist movements, foreign involvement, and many other causes would spur the development of extremely fundamentalist groups who would call for a strict separation of Sunni and Shia sects.

In this way, conflicts which largely arose out of other causes—political, economic, national, and so on—became redefined by these fundamentalist groups as a sectarian conflict between Sunni and Shia.

Iran and Iraq would be plunged into war as a result of border disputes and Iraq's desire to establish itself as the dominant state in the Gulf. This conflict was redrawn as one of Sunni vs. Shia because, while both nations contained a Shia majority, the government in Iraq was Sunni. They worried that the Iranian revolution in 1979 would spur an uprising by the Shia majority within their own borders. This would give Iran the upper hand and leave Iraq open to takeover by Iran.

Iran continues to exert its influence in Iraq as well as Syria, Lebanon, and Yemen by supporting Shia fundamentalist groups in those nations. As a result, Sunni and Shia have become increasingly divided. Where there were once mixed mosques in which Sunni and Shia would pray together, there is now heavy segregation, criticism, and even violence.

Saudi Arabia, a Sunni dominant nation, met with increasing disapproval by Iran and Shia groups for supporting Iraq during the war with Iran as well as for funding and providing weapons to Sunni militant groups in Pakistan and Afghanistan.

While the Sunni and Shia divide has increasingly been used to achieve political and economic goals—such as by Iran and Saudi Arabia—it is still not the root of the conflict. In fact, as we have seen in the chapters of this book, Sunni and Shia can and have lived together peacefully for thousands of years. Both Sunni and Shia fundamentalist groups make claims to a past conflict which either doesn't exist or is being greatly exaggerated.

The roots of the modern Sunni-Shia conflicts, then, are not found in the 1,400-year history but in the modern political and economic tensions that exist in the region. The majority of Muslims desire unity and peace rather than the domination of one group over the other.

While there have been attempts at achieving this unity, it is a difficult task in the face of the continued political and economic tensions. The path to unity and the resolution of the multiple entangled conflicts which have all become imagined as a single conflict between Sunni and Shia continues to be debated.

Some argue that the conflicts cannot be resolved until foreign interests—namely the United States and Europe—leave the Middle East. Others argue that if they were to leave, violence and fighting between the groups would only get worse. It is beyond the scope of this book to take a stance about how the situation could be resolved. However, it can safely be said that history proves unity and harmony between the two groups is possible.

Made in United States
North Haven, CT
12 May 2023

36499587R00036